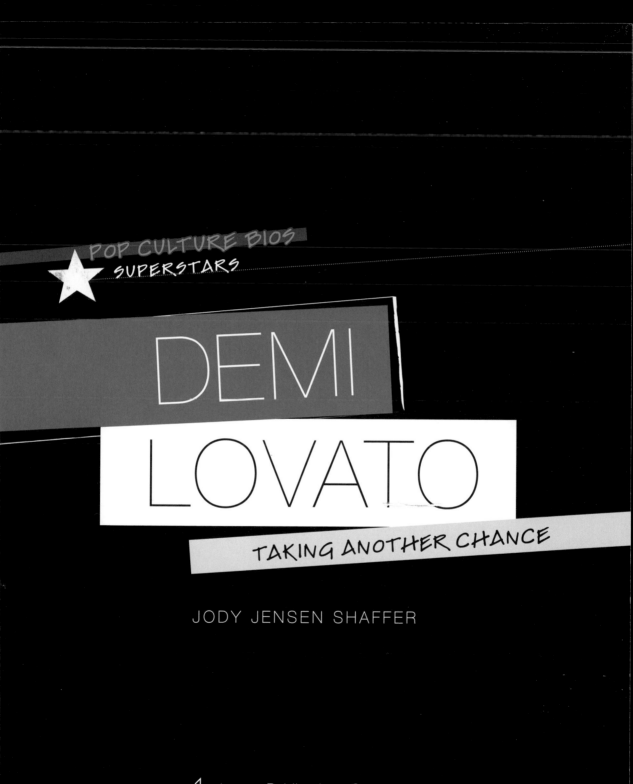

POP CULTURE BIOS
SUPERSTARS

DEMI

LOVATO

TAKING ANOTHER CHANCE

JODY JENSEN SHAFFER

Lerner Publications Company
MINNEAPOLIS

For Ann, Sue, Laura,
Michelle, and Deb

Lerner Publications Company
A division of Lerner Publishing Group, Inc.
241 First Avenue North
Minneapolis, MN 55401 U.S.A.

Website address: www.lernerbooks.com

Library of Congress Cataloging-in-Publication Data

Shaffer, Jody Jensen.
    Demi Lovato : taking another chance / by Jody Jensen
Shaffer.
        pages   cm. — (Pop culture bios: Superstars)
    Includes index.
    ISBN 978-1-4677-1310-8 (lib. bdg. : alk. paper)
    ISBN 978-1-4677-1770-0 (eBook)
    1. Lovato, Demi, 1992- —Juvenile literature. 2. Singers—
United States—Juvenile literature. 3. Actors—United States—
Biography—Juvenile literature. I. Title.
ML3930.L68S53 2014
791.4302'8092—dc23 [B]   2013001165

Manufactured in the United States of America
1 – BP – 7/15/13

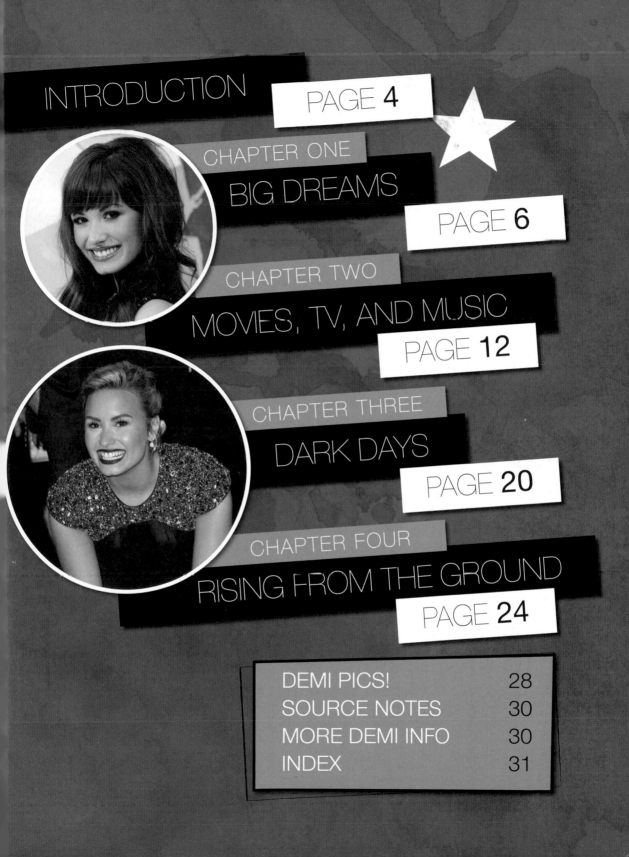

INTRODUCTION

Demi stops for a picture after winning the 2012 MTV Best Video with a Message award.

Demi Lovato struts down the red carpet in a glittery black dress and leather jacket. Hundreds of adoring fans— she calls them Lovatics—scream and reach for her. She dances to the stage, belting out the lyrics to her No. 1 single, "Give Your Heart a Break." Behind her, confetti shoots into the air. This is where Demi always wanted to be.

And even though she's performed hundreds of times, tonight is different. It's a new beginning. Demi has been nominated for MTV's 2012 Best Video with a Message award. It's for her video for "Skyscraper," a deeply personal song about her struggles and triumphs. Tonight is definitely one of Demi's triumphs.

Demi (RIGHT) and younger sister, Madison, are all smiles in 2011.

A young Demi poses for the camera in this family photo.

CHAPTER ONE

BIG DREAMS

Demi's sister Dallas (LEFT); stepfather, Eddie; and mother, Dianna, leave an airport in 2010.

Demetria Devonne Lovato was born on August 20, 1992, in Dallas, Texas. Her mom, Dianna, was a country music singer and one-time Dallas Cowboys cheerleader. Demi's dad, Patrick, played in a band.

Demi has two siblings. Dallas Lovato is about five years older than Demi. She's a TV and movie actress. Demi's younger half sister, Madison De La Garza, played Juanita Solis on the TV show *Desperate Housewives*.

Shortly after Demi turned two, her mom and dad divorced. Demi's mom later married Eddie De La Garza, whom Demi calls Dad. He managed a Ford dealership. In 2008, when Demi began to get famous, Eddie quit his job to help guide Demi's career.

Dallas (LEFT) and Demi show off flowers they picked in this adorable shot from the 1990s.

Demi & Friends

Demi always knew she wanted to perform. At the age of five, she sang "My Heart Will Go On" from the movie *Titanic*. "I sang at the kindergarten talent show," Demi remembers. **"It actually clicked in my head. I decided I wanted to be a singer."**

When Demi was almost eight, she auditioned for the TV show *Barney & Friends*. One of the other girls trying out was Selena Gomez. Demi's mom wasn't sure Demi would get a part. But the producers called her back for a second audition.

Demi and Selena both got roles. Demi

PRODUCER = a person who provides money and ideas for a movie or a TV show

This cast photo shows Demi (ON BLUE BALL) and Selena (ON YELLOW BALL) on the set of Barney in 2004.

played Angela. Selena was Gianna. The girls became BFFs right away. Demi appeared on seasons 7 and 8. When fifth grade ended in 2003, though, Demi had become too old for the show.

TAKE TWO

Demi actually auditioned for *Barney & Friends* twice. The first time, she was just five years old. She couldn't read yet, so she didn't get a part. The next time, she nailed it!

Demi Takes Lessons

After Demi's time on *Barney* ended, she focused on becoming a better performer. She had already taken piano lessons. Now she added guitar, singing, and acting lessons.

Demi was especially good at singing. Her voice teacher, Linda Septien, said Demi could sing the notes *between* the notes. She meant that as a giant compliment!

Demi also entered and won several beauty pageants. She loved to take to the stage in whatever way she could. She especially adored singing during the talent sections of the pageants.

Demi was a pageant star as a young girl.

When Demi was eight, she won the 2000 Texas State Cinderella Miniature Miss title.

Tough Times, Tough Girl

Despite Demi's success, life was sometimes hard for her. In sixth grade, she got bullied at school. Kids made fun of her weight. They broke her demo CDs. They sent her mean texts. Demi decided that she wanted to be homeschooled. Her mom agreed that this was a good idea. From then on, Demi never set foot in a school again. On April 23, 2009, she earned her high school diploma a year early.

DEMO CD = a recording used to give music producers an idea of how an artist sings

MUSICAL INSPIRATIONS

Demi loves all kinds of music, but she especially enjoys listening to Aretha Franklin (LEFT), Billie Holiday, Whitney Houston, Kelly Clarkson, and Christina Aguilera. The work of these artists has influenced Demi's own singing.

Although the bullying made her feel terrible, Demi didn't give up on her dreams. In 2006, her family moved to Los Angeles, California. Demi auditioned for parts in TV shows and commercials. One show she tried out for was Disney's *Hannah Montana*. She didn't get a part, but the producers liked her a lot.

Over the next two years, Demi scored guest appearances on the TV shows *Prison Break* and *Just Jordan*. Then, in 2007, Demi's hard work really paid off. She landed the role of Charlotte Adams on Disney's *As the Bell Rings*. Several of Demi's original songs played during the show.

Demi (THIRD FROM LEFT) and the cast of *As the Bell Rings* pose for a cast photo in 2008.

Demi (LEFT) and her best friend, Selena Gomez, strike a pose in 2009.

f family

CHAPTER TWO

MOVIES, TV, AND MUSIC

Demi scored super big in June of 2007. She auditioned for two Disney projects on the same day, the made-for-TV movie *Camp Rock* and the sitcom *Sonny with a Chance*. Amazingly, she won leading roles in both! Demi couldn't have been more thrilled.

Camp Rock

Within a week of her audition, Demi had hired a stylist and was writing songs for *Camp Rock*. In the film, Demi plays Mitchie Torres, a girl who goes to summer music camp. Demi costarred with Joe, Kevin, and Nick Jonas—better known as the Jonas Brothers!

Demi, Alyson Stoner (LEFT), and the Jonas Brothers attend a *Camp Rock* showing in 2008.

Demi worked extremely hard on the movie. "*Camp Rock* was my first movie, and in the first two weeks, I got really sick [from] exhaustion," Demi recalls. "I was in my trailer sweating. Drips of sweat were just coming off me because I was so stressed. It really does affect your health—how much you work, especially being this young." Demi leaned on her parents for support. **"I need[ed] them 24/7,"** she spilled.

Big Expectations

Buzz about *Camp Rock* began long before the movie aired. People thought Demi might be the next Miley Cyrus. Tons of magazines and newspapers ran stories about Demi.

Demi attended the *Camp Rock* premiere with her costars in New York City on June 11, 2008. Nine days later, *Camp Rock* debuted, and Demi's life changed forever. The movie was a massive hit. Nearly nine million people saw it the first night it was on. Four million viewers watched it the next day. *Camp Rock* was the biggest cable entertainment program of the year.

PREMIERE =
the first airing of a TV show or a movie. In a premiere, a show or a movie airs to a small, private audience before it is released to the public.

Sonny with a Chance

As if the frenzy following her film premiere wasn't enough, Demi also had loads of work to do for *Sonny with a Chance*. Demi was playing Sonny Munroe, a girl who wins a contest and gets to star in her favorite TV show. Demi spent hours practicing her lines and acting in episodes for the first season. The practice paid off. Disney viewers couldn't get enough of *Sonny*! The experience was fun but also challenging for Demi.

Demi and costar Tiffany Thornton take a break on the *Sonny with a Chance* set.

Demi works hard, but she also leaves time for a personal life. She has dated Cody Linley (RIGHT), Trace Cyrus (Miley's big bro), Joe Jonas, Wilmer Valderrama, and Niall Horan of the band One Direction.

Don't Forget

On top of all the acting, Demi was pouring effort into her singing career. In the summer of 2008, she toured with the Jonas Brothers. She was their opening act. She also recorded an album called *Don't Forget*. It came out on September 23. Several songs on the album were cowritten by the Jonas Brothers.

Demi's album debuted at No. 2 on the *Billboard* 200. Music lovers and critics raved about Demi's voice. Many thought she had stronger vocals than the Jonases!

Princess Protection Program

Demi took on a new acting project in 2009. She and BFF Selena reunited on-screen to star in Disney's *Princess Protection Program*. The movie was filmed in Puerto Rico. Demi and Sel had a blast taking in the sights of the island nation.

In the movie, Demi plays Rosalinda, a princess in hiding. She goes to live with regular teenager Carter Mason, played by Sel. The film showcased the ladies' offscreen friendship and their on-screen talent. Nearly 8.5 million people saw the film.

Demi (LEFT) and her BFF, Selena Gomez, costarred in Princess Protection Program in 2009. Demi played the princess. Selena played Carter Mason, a friend of the princess.

Here We Go Again

Just as she'd done in 2008, Demi juggled singing with her on-screen work. She announced her latest music news on Twitter on May 28, 2009. "Soon I will be shooting a music video for my single "Here We Go Again," Demi tweeted. **"[It's] from my new record, which will be released July 21ST!!!!!!!!!! YAYYY!"**

A TEXAS THANKSGIVING

On Thanksgiving Day 2008, Demi sang at the halftime show of the Dallas Cowboys football game. Millions of fans cheered her on, both in person at the game and in front of their TVs at home.

Demi's second album, *Here We Go Again*, debuted at No. 1 on the *Billboard* 200. Her single of the same title peaked at No. 15. It was Demi's first Top 10 hit as a solo artist. And Demi's success brought her even *more* success. She got to headline her own tour. She visited forty-seven cities in the summer of 2009.

Camp Rock 2: The Final Jam

In 2010, Demi was back at camp with the Jonases. They acted together in *Camp Rock 2: The Final Jam*. The cast loved being reunited for this new film. When they weren't filming, they went go-carting and miniature golfing.

The movie aired on September 3, 2010. Nearly 8 million fans watched it. The sound track came out in August. It debuted at No. 3 on the *Billboard* 200.

Demi hit the road again with the Jonas Brothers for

their Live in Concert World Tour. It kicked off on August 10. They played cities in the United States, Canada, Mexico, and South America.

When she wasn't touring, Demi was back in the TV studio, doing more filming for *Sonny with a Chance*. In October, the sound track for that show was released. Demi sang four songs on the album.

Demi joins Joe Jonas for a song on their 2010 tour.

CHAPTER THREE

DARK DAYS

Demi and her mom share a happy moment in 2009.
Demi's mom helped her through her dark days.

In late October 2010, the frantic pace of Demi's life and the pressures of stardom began to catch up with her. **"I went from movie to album to touring to television and back,"** Demi noted. "Being in the limelight wasn't the root of my problems, but it didn't help. I never took more than two weeks off in four years."

While traveling with the Jonas Brothers in South America, Demi had to leave the tour. She checked herself into a treatment center in Lemont, Illinois. She knew she needed help dealing with the stress she was experiencing. She had begun to react to the stress in some very dangerous ways. She admits that she'd started using drugs during this time. She also struggled with an eating disorder. In addition, she was cutting, or making cuts on her own skin on purpose. Cutting is a way that some people try to deal with painful feelings. But it can lead to serious injuries. Demi knew she had to stop.

Being in treatment was "really, really hard and scary," remembers Demi. "I was homesick and lonely." She thought about leaving sometimes. But her mom would remind her how important it was for her to get better. Demi listened to her mom and stayed.

EATING DISORDER = a health condition that causes abnormal eating. For example, someone with an eating disorder may not eat enough because he or she fears being overweight or is struggling with emotional issues.

While in treatment, Demi learned she has bipolar disorder. This illness causes people to go back and forth between very happy moods and very sad moods. It can make dealing with stress extra hard. It helped explain why Demi reacted as she did to the stress of performing.

Demi was relieved to find out she had bipolar. She finally understood why she sometimes felt so bad. She started to learn some healthful ways to deal with her feelings. And slowly, she started to feel better.

Demi returned to Los Angeles in late January 2011. "I'm not saying I'm perfect or fixed, but I am learning to love and accept myself," she explained. **"My outlook is more positive and I am happy."**

Demi decided not to return to *Sonny*. She was sad to leave the show. But she knew she shouldn't take things too quickly as she recovered.

Demi spent the next several months relaxing and reflecting on what she wanted to do next. "I didn't know if I'd be able to go back to work, but...I couldn't see myself going to college or working nine-to-five," she noted. She resolved to just enjoy her downtime and to take things as they came.

THINGS THAT MAKE DEMI HAPPY

caramel-filled Hershey's Kisses
the clothing stores Forever 21, Aldo, and Topshop
the band Paramore
the movie *Donnie Darko*
hanging out with her mom

"Skyscraper"

As Demi recovered, her lifestyle got more and more healthful. She stopped hanging out with people who weren't good for her. She began exercising and eating balanced meals.

Demi accepts her People's Choice Award in 2012. Presenters Josh Hutcherson and Vanessa Hudgens look on.

By summer, Demi decided she was ready to go back to work. On July 12, 2011, she released her song called "Skyscraper." The song was very personal for Demi. In it, she compares herself to a skyscraper rising from the ground.

Demi recorded other songs along with "Skyscraper." On September 20, 2011, she released the songs on an album called *Unbroken*. Her fans loved it. In January of 2012, Demi won the People's Choice Award for Favorite Pop Artist.

Demi released her second single from the album, "Give Your Heart a Break," in late January. By August, it had been certified platinum. That meant it had sold more than one million copies. The next month, it reached No. 1 on the *Billboard* Pop 100. Demi was back in the music scene. But more importantly, she was getting stronger and happier every day.

Demi poses with Simon Cowell—the tough vocal critic whom many love to hate!

CHAPTER FOUR

RISING FROM THE GROUND

Demi adds her handprints to the concrete in front of TCL Chinese Theatre in Hollywood.

In 2012, Demi decided that she didn't want to keep her problems private. She instead wanted to use them to help others. She released an MTV film about her time in treatment called *Demi Lovato: Stay Strong*. She became the anti-bullying spokesperson for a group called PACER (Parent Advocacy Coalition for Educational Rights). And she signed on as a contributing editor to *Seventeen*. Demi writes about personal issues for the magazine as part of a campaign called "Love Is Louder Than the Pressure to Be Perfect."

Becoming a judge on *The X Factor* was a highlight for Demi in 2012. She joined judges (FROM LEFT) L. A. Reid, Britney Spears, and Simon Cowell.

Demi is also Secret deodorant's ambassador against bullying. As part of their Mean Stinks campaign, Demi visited a Harlem, New York, girls' school in September. She told the girls, "Mean girls aren't cool. [Bullying] doesn't make you popular. I hate bullies. You know what I love? I love girls who want to gang up for good, that want to have a drama-free time in their school." She told the students to speak up if they were being bullied. **"Remember that you're all beautiful,"** she advised.

Demi surprises students in New York as part of an anti-bullying assembly in 2012.

CELL SILENCE

At one time, Demi felt too attached to her cell phone. So she didn't use it for three months! What did she do instead? She talked to people face-to-face. Epic.

Stronger Than Ever

These days, Demi is stronger than ever. Her future seems as bright as her smile. Her career is headed in just one direction: up! And she dreams of getting married and having children someday.

Demi promises to keep on writing and singing songs for her fans. **"When you work really hard at something, eventually, it pays off,"** she says. **"No matter what it is."**

What type of guy would Demi eventually like to marry? Someone cute who makes her laugh. The only deal breaker? Someone who is controlling. She'd *never* put up with that!

DEMI
PICS!

SOURCE NOTES

8   Robert Wilonsky, "Disney Channel Fits Colleyville's Demi Lovato for a Glass Slipper," *Dallas Observer,* May 29, 2008, http://www.dallasobserver.com/content/printVersion/985871/ (April 9, 2013).

14 Ibid.

17 Demi Lovato, Twitter, posted on May 28, 2009, https://twitter.com/ddlovato/status/1957085257 (April 9, 2013).

21 Antonia Hoyle, "The Fame, the Drugs, the Self-Harm," *Fabulous,* April 22, 2012, http://fabulousmag.co.uk/2012/04/22/the-fame-the-drugs-the-self-harm/ (April 9, 2013).

21 Ibid.

22 Ibid.

22 Ibid

26 Jennifer Cunningham, "Demi Tough Lovato Smacks Down Bullying on E. Harlem Visit," *New York Daily News,* September 21, 2012.

27 Wilonsky, "Disney Channel."

MORE DEMI INFO

Demi Lovato Official Site
http://www.demilovato.com
On Demi's site, you can download her music, buy Demi merchandise, and get the official Demi Lovato mobile app.

Demi on Twitter
https://twitter.com/DDLovato
Follow Demi as she dishes about what she's doing, where she's going, and whom she's seeing.

Demi on YouTube
http://www.youtube.com/user/DemiLovatoVEVO
Watch Demi perform all her latest hit songs.

Nelson, Robin. *Selena Gomez: Pop Star and Actress*. Minneapolis: Lerner Publications Company, 2013.
Read all about Demi's BFF Selena.

Rajczak, Kristen. *Demi Lovato*. New York: Gareth Stevens, 2012.
Find out more about Demi in this fun book.

INDEX

The images in this book are used with the permission of: © Jason LaVeris/FilmMagic/Getty Images, pp. 2, 27; © Scott Gries/Getty Images, pp. 3 (top), 12 (bottom left); © FeatureFlash/ImageCollect, pp. 3 (bottom), 24 (left); AP Photo/Matt Sayles/Invision, p. 4 (top); CFI/Splash News/Newscom, p. 4 (bottom); © Kevin Mazur/WireImage/Getty Images, p. 5; © Alberto E. Rodriguez/Getty Images, p. 6 (top left); © Patrick Lovato/Zuma Wire Service/Alamy, pp. 6 (top right), 7; Sharky/Splash News/Newscom, p. 6 (bottom); © Hit Entertainment/Courtesy Everett Collection, p. 8; © ZUMA Wire Service/Alamy, p. 9; © Rick Diamond/Getty Images for The Fox Theatre, p. 10; © Bob D'Amico/Disney Channel/Courtesy Everett Collection, p. 11; © George Pimentel/WireImage/Getty Images, p. 12 (top); Clasos/Splash News/Newscom, p. 12 (bottom right); © Ferdaus Shamim/WireImage/Getty Images, p. 13; © Adam Rose/Disney Channel via Getty Images, p. 15; © S_buckley/ImageCollect, p. 16; W.Disney/Everett/Rex USA, p. 17; © Todd Strand/Independent Picture Service, pp. 18, 22; © Jamie McCarthy/WireImage/Getty Images, p. 19; Kevin Crowley/Splash News/Newscom, p. 20 (top); Hot Shots Worldwide/Newscom, p. 20 (bottom); Mario Anzuoni/Reuters/Newscom, p. 23; AP Photo/Rex Features/Rob Latour, p. 24 (right); © Photo by Fox via Getty Images, p. 25; AP Photo/MediaPunch/Rex Features, p. 26; © Michael Tran/FilmMagic/Getty Images, pp. 28 (top left), 29 (bottom); © Byron Purvis/AdMedia/ImageCollect, p. 28 (right); AP Photo/John Shearer/Invision, p. 28 (bottom left); © Russ Elliot/AdMedia/ImageCollect, p. 29 (top left); © Kevin Brooks/AdMedia/ImageCollect, p. 29 (right); © Steve Granitz/WireImage/Getty Images, p. 29 (top middle).

Front cover: © Helga Esteb/Shutterstock.com (main); © Jason Merritt/WireImage/Getty Images (inset). Back cover: © Steve Granitz/WireImage/Getty Images.

Main body text set in Shannon Std Book 12/18.
Typeface provided by Monotype Typography.